DEDUCT IT! DEDUCT IT! 2018 ORDER FORM

ORDERING METHODS:

1. Order at Web site: BertWhitehead.com — select *Bert's Bookstore*
2. Mail order form with credit card information or check/money order payable to:

   Bert Whitehead, LLC
   111 Willits #205
   Birmingham, MI 48009

3. Fax order to: 248-737-8010   ♦*May also be purchased at Amazon.com or the NATP Tax Store*

BERT'S BOOKSTORE QUANTITIES/PRICES:

QUANTITY:	SHIPPING/HANDLING:
One..........$9.95	Up to $19.99....$2.95
2-10..........$9.00/each	$20 - $49.99.....$4.95
11-20........$8.00/each	$50 - $89.99.....$7.95
21-50........$7.00/each	$90 - $159.99...$12.95
51-249......$6.00/each	$160+...............$19.95

Requested Quantity _____ at _____ each   Subtotal _____ + S/H _____ = $ _____ TOTAL

METHOD OF PAYMENT

☐ Cash   ☐ Check   ☐ Credit Card

CREDIT CARD NO. ☐☐☐☐ ☐☐☐☐ ☐☐☐☐ ☐☐☐☐

EXPIRATION DATE ☐☐/☐☐   3 OR 4 DIGIT CODE ☐☐☐☐   AMOUNT ☐☐☐☐☐

X_____
PLEASE PRINT NAME AS IT APPEARS ON CARD

X_____
CARD MEMBER'S SIGNATURE

BILLING/SHIPPING INFORMATION (as it appears on your credit card):

Name	
Billing Address	
City, State, ZIP	
Phone	Email Address

SHIPPING ADDRESS (if different from the billing address):

Name	
Billing Address	
City, State, ZIP	
Phone	Email Address
Questions or Quantity over 250?	Send a message to deductittracker@yahoo.com or call 800-224-1040 ext. 101

Copyright © 2018 by Carol Johnson and Bert Whitehead

All rights reserved. Information herein is a compilation of many resources and not a guarantee. Fair market value may vary based on region. No part of this book shall be reproduced or transmitted in any form or by any means, electronic, mechanical, magnetic, or photographic including photocopying, recording or by any information storage and retrieval system, without prior written permission of the authors. No patent liability is assumed with respect to the use of the information contained herein. Although every precaution has been taken in the preparation of this book, the authors assume no responsibility for errors or omissions. Neither is any liability assumed for damages resulting from the use of the information contained herein.

This publication is designed to provide accurate and authoritative information in regard to the subject matter covered. It is sold with the understanding that the authors are not engaged in rendering legal, accounting, or investment advice, or any other professional service to the reader. If legal advice or other expert assistance is required, the services of a competent professional person should be sought.

Deduct It! Deduct It! For Tax Year 2018
ISBN 978-1-5323-6582-9

Deduct It! Deduct It!:	Copyright 2006-2018
Type of Work:	Text
Application Title:	Deduct It! Deduct It! For 2018 Tax Year.
Description:	Book, 108 p.
Copyright Claimant:	Carol Johnson, 1955- .
	Bert Whitehead, JD, 1944- .
Date of Creation:	January 2018
Date of Publication:	January 2018
Nation of First Publication:	United States
Authorship on Application:	Carol Johnson, 1955- ; Citizenship: United States. Authorship: text, compilation, editing
	Bert Whitehead, JD, 1944- ; Citizenship: United States. Authorship: editing.
Pre-existing Material:	artwork.
Basis of Claim:	text, compilation, editing.

Printed in the United States by Edwards Brothers Malloy℠

Contactd Info: DEDUCT IT! DEDUCT IT!
Bert Whitehead, LLC
111 Willits #205
Birmingham, MI 48009
800-224-1040
DeductItTracker@Yahoo.com

CONTENTS

Foreword 1

Deduct It! Deduct It! Assurance 3

How to Give 4

How to 'Steps' 5

How to Details 6

The "How's" of Valuing your Donation

    Fair Market Value 8

    Receipts 8

    Qualified Appraisals 9

What to Give 10

Donating Special Items

    Designer Items 10

    Items Not Listed, Collectibles, and Antiques 10

    Mileage and Other Items You Should Track 11

Where to Donate 12

Tax Preparation:
Submitting Your Charitable Donation to the IRS 14

If You're Audited 15

    We'll Stand Behind You 15

Why Donate? 16

Substantiating Non-cash Contributions to Charity 16

Tracking Multiple Donations 17

CONTENTS (Continued)

Contribution Record 18
    Clothing 19-27
    Outerwear 28-30
    Accessories 31
    Footwear 32-33
    Maternity 34
    Baby & Toddler 35-39
    Household and Kitchen Items
        Crafts 40
        Dry Goods 41-43
        Decor 44-45
        Electronics 46-49
        Entertainment 50
        Garden/Lawn 51
        Kitchen 52-55
        Luggage 56
        Musical Instruments 57-58
        Pets 59
        Workshop 60
    Sports Equipment, Exercise Equipment, Toys and Video Games
        Sports & Exercise Equipment 61-65
        Toys 66
        Video Games/Systems 67-68

CONTENTS (Continued)

Furniture & Medical 69-73

Appliances 74-75

Computer and Peripherals 76-77

Designer Items 78

Your Page: Items not Listed
   (Vintage, Custom, Unique, Designer, Other) 79-85

Deduct It! Deduct It! Totals 86-89

Charitable Mileage and Out-of-Pocket Expenses 90

Beyond the Closet:
Other Types of Charitable Donations 91-93

Documentation Records 94-96

Notes 97-98

Online and Other Resources 99

Charity Verification Tracker 100

DEDUCT IT! DEDUCT IT!
FEEDBACK / CORRECTIONS / COMMENTS

Please feel free to email: DeductItTracker@yahoo.com

or

Fax to: 248-737-8010

Let us know what changes would make this booklet more helpful to you next year!

PAGE	FEEDBACK

OTHER FEEDBACK:

A Word from the Authors

Deduct It! Deduct It! was developed as a convenient way to document charitable donations while you're boxing them up. Most methods now use computer software, so you have to write down your donation, call up the software and type it in, in effect doubling your work.

We continue to do extensive research into the new rules from the IRS on charitable contributions and our program meets all IRS regulations. As an indicator of value, the "fair market value" amounts we list have been researched in the later months of 2017 and early 2018 across the country in thrift & used clothing stores, second hand shops, and auction websites. Enjoy this organized, easy to follow process and obtain the deduction you have coming to you for your non-cash charitable donations. All you may need is a calculator at year-end to add up your tax savings!

Carol Johnson and Bert Whitehead

DISCLAIMER: We are only summarizing the general rules for more common non-cash contributions, and you should review IRS Publication 526 for more complete details. For issues not addressed, especially if the contribution is large, it would be prudent to discuss with a tax professional who is knowledgeable about your situation. In particular, contributions of appreciated securities to a charity or transfer of a Required Minimum Distribution from an IRA to a charity should be reviewed by a professional before the contribution is made to assure that it is done correctly. The following information is intended to provide general guidance about the IRS rules regarding donations of non-cash items and is not a substitute for professional counsel. Consult your tax or legal advisor for professional guidance.

Foreword

Bert Whitehead, JD, MBA, is a fee-only personal financial advisor and tax attorney. He began his career in 1972, pioneering the Cambridge System™, a holistic approach that helps everyday people manage their financial lives. His firm specializes in the preparation of individual tax returns, and we've utilized their extensive knowledge of the U.S. tax law in the development of this book.

Carol Johnson, RP® is a Registered (financial) Paraplanner through the College of Financial Planning. She holds several certificates in ISO and Six Sigma, and is the development and detail person behind *Deduct It! Deduct It!*

Why is the bird on the front cover squawking "Deduct It, Deduct It"? Some years ago, Bert acquired a pet cockatiel that lived in the office. Bert and Ernie, the pair of characters on the children's show *Sesame Street*, naturally were the inspiration for Bert dubbing the bird "Ernie."

Ernie was taught a single phrase: "Deduct It, Deduct It!" Tax season must have been quite noisy in those days, but when we came up with the idea for this book, Ernie's call gave us our title.

Bert continues to practice his style of holistic fee-only financial planning today. He founded the nonprofit Alliance of Comprehensive Planners in 1995 which has trained over 300 fee-only financial advisors across the country. He is the author of *Why Smart People Do Stupid Things with Money: Overcoming Financial Dysfunction*, and is recognized nationally by the media.

For more information and to access Bert's Bookstore, visit:

bertwhitehead.com

Consumers

To find a fee-only holistic financial advisor in your area, select "Find an ACP Planner" at acplanners.org

Advisors

If you would like to learn more about the Alliance of Comprehensive Planners and becoming a fee-only financial advisor, select "Be an ACP Planner" at acplanners.org

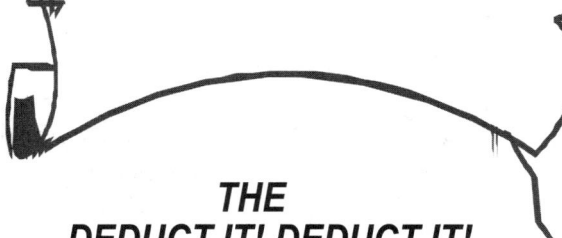

THE DEDUCT IT! DEDUCT IT! ASSURANCE

Completion of this book, as instructed, provides all required documentation to substantiate a legitimate deduction, including inventory corroborated by photos, receipts from the charity, and appraisals where required of the inventory of items given.

We have performed the due diligence generally required to establish estimated fair market value of listed items.

■ HOW TO GIVE

PLEASE

- Wash or dry-clean clothing.
- Test electrical equipment and battery-operated items. Include the manual whenever possible.
- Include all pieces and parts to children's games and toys.
- Verify your charity will accept computers, mattresses, window blinds, appliances, or other bulky/unique items.
- Tack a note on highly valued designer items with the approximate year and amount paid so the charity is sure to price it to their best benefit.

PLEASE DON'T

- Don't leave items unattended outside the donation center or at drop boxes without attendants to give you a receipt.
- Don't donate broken or soiled items.
- Don't give items that don't meet current safety standards, or that have been recalled or banned.

■ HOW-TO STEPS

1. Gather your donations.
2. Take photos of items sorted/stacked by type.
3. Document them using the "Contribution Record" section beginning on page 19.
4. Take a picture of your entire boxed/bagged donation.
5. Take your donation to a local drop-off center or call a charity for pickup.
6. Complete the details (name/address/etc.) necessary to support your tax deduction (page 100).

6a. For added "audit protection" you can use the "Charity Verification Tracker" on the last page of the book and have the charity attendant initial the detail box you've filled out for this donation.

6b. You can also take a picture of your entire donation at the 'donation drop-off' door of the charity. If you have arranged a pick up, take a picture of the boxed/bagged donation on your porch or curbside. Remember to get a receipt!

■ HOW-TO DETAILS

1. Gather your donations.
Annual charitable contributions of clothing and other household articles can add up to a significant tax deduction and at the same time help those in need.

2. Sort items by Type and take photos.
It is especially important to take photographs of your charitable donation. A photo of each item is not necessary, just arrange them so each item is visible. If you use a digital camera, simply print out your pictures or save electronically — but be prepared to print them out in the event you are audited. Our recommendation is a quick printout tucked into the back of this book.

3. Document your items.
Go to pages 19 through 85 and document your items on the Deduct It! donation tables. IRS guidelines state FMV (Fair Market Value) will be estimated by you. The Deduct It! Deduct It! tracker will guide you with current estimates of FMV from various sources across the U.S.

4. Take a Picture of Your Entire Boxed/Bagged Donation.
During an Audit, the IRS sometimes requests more proof that the items were truly donated.

5. Deliver or arrange pickup of your contribution.

6. More Pictures and get a receipt!
If possible, take a picture of your donation at the Charity while the boxes/bags/furniture is being accepted. If you've arranged pickup, take a picture of the charity loading their truck.

If you can't/don't get a receipt, you can't get a deduction!
The receipt must include:

- The organization's name
- The date of the donation
- The amount of the contribution (valued by you)

7. Take care of the details to support your tax deduction.

- Log who you donated the items to on page 100. Code your photos A, B, C, D as directed.

- Tuck, paperclip, or staple the picture(s) and receipt into your Deduct It! Deduct It! book.

- At tax time, add up your contributions. Use the total on page 89 for your tax preparer. Be sure to bring any Qualified Appraisals* as they must be sent in with your tax return.

- File Deduct It! Deduct It! with your tax preparation supportive paperwork.

*See page 9: "Qualified Appraisals" for details.

THE 'HOWS' OF VALUING YOUR DONATION

Fair Market Value

Fair market value (FMV) is the price that property would sell for on the open market. It is the price that would be agreed on between a willing buyer and a willing seller, with neither being required to act, and both having reasonable knowledge of the relevant facts. (IRS Publication 561).

For example, if you donate used clothing to the local Salvation Army or Goodwill store, a number of factors come into play when you're calculating the FMV. It can vary from region to region, and you'll need to consider the condition of the item as well as its appeal to a potential buyer. The burden of proof is on you, the taxpayer, to value the item. And clearly it's to your benefit neither to undervalue nor overvalue your charitable donations. FMV will be considerably less than the price you paid for the item new.

When calculating the FMV, you must consider the age, manufacturer, brand, condition and original purchase price of each donated article. *The FMV shown in this book is a general range based on used items.* Congress has clamped down on donations of household goods to stop people from inflating the value of their used items.

Better (High)	Shows little to no wear
Good (Low)	Slightly used or worn

Receipts

Whether you deliver or have your donation picked up, the charity will give you a receipt. Although it is up to you to document the FMV of your donation, the receipt validates the donation (but usually does not itemize the goods or put a value on them).

Always get a receipt! The larger the value of your donation, the more you're throwing away. If you itemize deductions and are in a 32% tax bracket, and you put the equivalent of $1,500 FMV of clothing into an unmanned bin, you just threw away $480!

■ QUALIFIED APPRAISALS

If your total deduction for all non-cash contributions for the year is over $500, you must complete and attach IRS Form 8283, Non-cash Charitable Contributions, to your tax return. Taxpayers donating an item or a group of similar items valued at more than $5,000 must also complete Section B of Form 8283, which requires an appraisal by a qualified appraiser.

Hire a professional appraiser to determine the value of your donation if the individual clothing item or outfit, or furniture, is worth more than $500 or items/groups of similar items over $5,000 (this applies to any non-cash donation). The appraiser must have authorization to complete Section B, Part III of Form 8283 and you must file a declaration of appraisal with the form. Appraisers familiar with IRS requirements may be found at appraisers.org.

The "good or better" rule does not apply with items over $500. If you have a "poor" condition single item that a qualified appraiser values over $500, you may donate it.

You may not take a charitable contribution deduction for fees you pay for appraisals of your donated property. However, these fees may qualify as a miscellaneous deduction, subject to the 2% limit, on Schedule A (Form 1040) if paid to determine the amount allowable as a charitable contribution.

WHAT TO GIVE

> -IRS definition of a charitable contribution-
> "a donation or gift to a qualified organization that is both voluntary and made without getting, or expecting to get, anything of equal value".

Charities are looking for all sorts of clothing, household items, small appliances, toys, and tools to sell. Large furniture pieces, appliances, copiers, metal desks, carpeting, and used mattresses are (sometimes and regretfully) too costly to handle and/or repair. Please call ahead or check their website for acceptable vs. unacceptable donations.

If you're donating jewelry, gems, collections, paintings, antiques, other objets d'art, cars, land, buildings, intellectual property, etc., special rules and regulations apply. They are listed in IRS Publication 561 "Determining the Value of Donated Property". We recommend you consult your financial advisor or tax preparer.

DONATING SPECIAL ITEMS

Designer Items

Designer items have a higher FMV than typical or everyday articles of clothing or household goods. Name-brand and designer clothing must have the sewn-in label intact.

Items Not Listed, Collectibles and Antiques

These items are unique, and it is appropriate to value them individually. The final list called "Your Page" in the Contribution Record section includes blank lines for you to describe and value items not listed in Deduct It! Deduct It!, designer items, collectibles and antiques. Keep in mind that the FMV of these items may be determined by:

- Searching similar items on eBay using filters 'Completed Listings' and 'Sold Items'.
- Searching craigslist.org, or auction sites
- Similar items at local thrift, resale shops or garage sales
- Catalogs for collectibles
- Qualified appraisals (necessary for single items over $500 or items/groups of similar items over $5,000)

Mileage and Other Items You Should Track

Out-of-pocket costs for individuals volunteering for 501(c)3 charitable organizations are deductible.

The mileage rate for charitable miles is set by statute (not the IRS) and remains at $.14 per mile for 2018.

350 miles adds up to a $49 tax deduction. It doesn't take too many trips to drop off donations, driving for a religious organization or the Boy Scouts to really add up!

Although the value of volunteer time or services to a charitable organization is not deductible, some costs incurred are. So, be sure to keep track of out-of-pocket expenses while providing volunteer work (e.g., purchasing Sunday school supplies, postage, telephone costs). There are a variety of restrictions, so review this with your tax preparer and/or review IRS Publication 526.

Whether you're sorting through items in your closet, garage, or kitchen, you'll be able to carry Deduct It! Deduct It! with you to jot down what you're donating. All of your information will be in one place, so at tax time you won't be digging through a stack of papers on your desk or a box full of receipts.

WHERE TO DONATE

If you know a needy individual and you give assistance directly to them, you can't deduct any part of the donation. You must give to a qualified charitable organization.

The IRS has an excellent interactive webpage called "Exempt Organizations Select Check" at:

irs.gov/Charities-&-Non-Profits/Exempt-Organizations-Select-Check

It has a powerful search feature that will help you locate as the IRS explains, "organizations to which contributions are deductible as a charitable donation (as defined in section 170 of the Internal Revenue Code). It's also available in IRS Publication 78. Another option is to ask the organization or call the local IRS office for your organization's "Letter of Determination."

IRS Publication 526 gives you a quick checklist to help you sort out deductible versus nondeductible contributions:

DEDUCTIBLE AS CHARITABLE CONTRIBUTIONS	NOT DEDUCTIBLE AS CHARITABLE CONTRIBUTIONS
Money or property you give to: • Churches, synagogues, temples, mosques, and other religious organizations • Federal, state, and local governments, if your contribution is solely for public purposes (for example, a gift to reduce the public debt) • Nonprofit schools and hospitals • Public parks and recreation facilities • Salvation Army, Red Cross, CARE, Goodwill Industries, United Way, Boy Scouts, Girl Scouts, Boys and Girls Clubs of America, etc. • War veterans' groups Expenses paid for a student living with you, sponsored by a qualified organization Out-of-pocket expenses when you serve a qualified organization as a volunteer	Money or property you give to: • Civic leagues, social and sports clubs, labor union, and chambers of commerce • Foreign organizations (except certain Canadian, Israeli, and Mexican charities) • Groups that are run for personal profit • Groups whose purpose is to lobby for law changes • Homeowner's associations • Individuals • Political groups or candidates for public office Cost of raffle, bingo, or lottery tickets Dues, fees, or bills paid to country clubs, lodges, fraternal orders, or similar groups Tuition Value of your time or services Value of blood given at a blood bank

Source: IRS Publication 526, "Charitable Contributions"

Deduct It! Deduct It! will help you track the non-cash donations you make to qualified 501(c)(3) organizations.

TAX PREPARATION - Submitting your Charitable Deduction to the IRS

In order to deduct your charitable contributions, you must itemize your deductions on your tax return. You'll itemize if your total itemized deductions are greater than the standard deduction ($24,000 on joint returns, $18,000 head of household, and $12,000 on single returns/married filing separately for 2018). We've heard Congress has looked into a charitable deduction for non-itemizers, but a provision to that effect has not been passed. However, charitable contributions, including non-cash items, still count as deductions even for people who are subject to AMT (the Alternate Minimum Tax).

You get the tax deduction in the same year you make the contribution. Donations are often made by December 31 in order to qualify for the deduction. You'll include the total donation on your Individual Tax Return (Line 17 of Schedule A). Keep your completed Deduct It! Deduct It! book (including receipts and photographs) with your backup tax preparation records. It will substantiate your contributions in the event of an audit.

You must file Form 8283, "Non-Cash Charitable Contributions," with your tax return if your cumulative donations are over $500 in one year (that's all the clothing, shoes, household items, etc. added up). The form asks for the method used to determine the FMV (fair market value). Indicate "thrift shop values".

There are some special limitations on the deductible amounts which can be found in IRS Publication 526 "Charitable Deductions". We recommend you discuss this with your tax preparer or financial advisor.

IF YOU'RE AUDITED
(On Your Charitable Goods Contribution)

1. Stay calm – your income tax return being selected for audit does not mean "they are out to get you!" Often times the computer has randomly selected your return as part of a routine audit program. The IRS will tell you the items they have selected for audit.
2. Contact your tax professional, if you have one.
3. Your Deduct It! Deduct It! book with receipts, pictures, verifications, and appraisals (if appropriate) attached suffice to support your non-cash contributions.

WE'LL STAND BEHIND YOU!

If you are audited on your charitable goods contribution and the IRS agent questions the validity of our Fair Market Values, please contact us!

Ask your preparer to contact us or send us a copy of the Audit Notification you received from the IRS specifying non-cash contributions as part of your audit. Include your email or street address and we'll send you the information. This document will substantiate the FMV (fair market estimated values) which we have listed.

Scan your notification and Email to: deductittracker@yahoo.com
Fax to: 248-737-8010 or write:
Deduct It! Deduct It!
Bert Whitehead, LLC
111 Willits, #205
Birmingham, MI 48009
800-224-1040

▪ WHY DONATE?

The agencies you donate to are able to profit from your generosity, helping them help others. Feel comfortable knowing your charitable contributions are good for society.

Deduct It! Deduct It! gives you the details on how to document and maximize your charitable donation according to IRS guidelines, so think of it lowering your tax bill.

▪ WHAT IT MEANS TO YOU

Donating Clothing and/or Household Goods

Your Marginal Tax Bracket	Clothing/Good Contribution	Tax Savings
24%	$500	$120
35%	$500	$175
24%	$1,000	$240
35%	$1,000	$350

Substantiating Non-Cash Contributions to Charity

Use this booklet all through the year (each time) you gather up a charitable donation. If you give multiple times, we recommend you pick up several of these books. Documenting will be easier, and the cost of the books will be minimal compared to your properly documented and valued donation!

Be sure to bring Deduct It! Deduct It! with you in 2019 when you have your 2018 taxes prepared. Your financial advisor or tax preparer is going to see an organized and appropriately valued charitable donation for use on IRS Schedule A and/or Form 8283.

Donating an item not listed in Deduct It! Deduct It!?
See page 78 for details.

Tracking Multiple Donations -

The Deduct It Tracker is set up for four (4) donations (see pages 86 – 89 and 100 to review the "A, B, C, D" method for tracking each donation).

You may tally your donation each time matching against your photos. If this doesn't work for you, you could use a different color pen for each donation, or circle your "A" donation, put a square around your "B" donation, a cloud around your "C" donation and leave your "D" donation blank.

Want more ease in documenting your donations? Try using a separate Deduct It! Deduct It! book for each donation.

CONTRIBUTION RECORD

Clothing..19-27
Outerwear..28-30
Accessories...31
Footwear..32-33
Maternity...34
Baby & Toddler Gear...35-39
Household and Kitchen Items
    Crafts..40
    Dry Goods..41-43
    Decor..44-45
    Electronics..46-49
    Entertainment..50
    Garden/Lawn..51
    Kitchen...52-55
    Luggage...56
    Musical Instruments...57-58
    Pets..59
    Workshop..60
Sports and Exercise..61-65
Toys...66
Video Game Systems..67-68
Furniture & Medical..69-73
Appliances..74-75
Computers and Peripherals....................................76-77
Designer Item Needing Qualified Appraisals...............78
Your Page: Items not Listed
  (Vintage, Custom, Unique, Designer, Other)......79-85

CONTRIBUTION RECORD

CLO

For help with valuing your donations, see tips shown on page 78.	Gender	Qty	FMV better (high range)	Qty	FMV good (low range)	Your Total FMV	Estimate Original Purchase Price (Total)	Approx. Year Acquired
CLOTHING								
Bathing Suit	GIRL		$13.00		$3.00			
Bathing Suit - designer (e.g. Burberry, Speedo)	GIRL		$30.00		$6.00			
Bathing Suit/swim trunks	BOY		$21.00		$3.00			
Bathing Suit	WOM		$21.00		$5.00			
Bathing Suit - designer (e.g. Burberry, Prada, Juicy Couture)	WOM		$80.00		$8.00			
Bathing Suit/swim trunks	MEN		$24.00		$3.00			
Bathrobe	GIRL		$18.00		$3.00			
Bathrobe	BOY		$15.00		$3.00			
Bathrobe	WOM		$43.00		$4.00			
Bathrobe	MEN		$49.00		$5.00			
Blazer/Jacket	WOM		$24.00		$5.00			
							← TOTAL FOR PAGE 19	

CLO

CONTRIBUTION RECORD

For help with valuing your donations, see tips shown on page 78.	Gender	Qty	FMV better (high range)	Qty	FMV good (low range)	Your Total FMV	Estimate Original Purchase Price (Total)	Approx. Year Acquired
Blazer/ Business Jackets - designer (e.g. Escada, Misook)	WOM		$130.00		$10.00			
Blouses	GIRL		$28.00		$2.00			
Blouse/Shirt - desginer (e.g. Burberry)	CHILD		$32.00		$8.00			
Blouse - casual long sleeve	WOM		$20.00		$4.00			
Blouse - casual short sleeve	WOM		$19.00		$3.00			
Blouse - cotton top (long, 3/4 or short sleeve)	WOM		$23.00		$4.00			
Blouse - dress/work long sleeve	WOM		$32.00		$3.00			
Blouse - dress/work short sleeve	WOM		$22.00		$4.00			
Blouse - tank top	WOM		$24.00		$4.00			
Bras/unique/stylish	WOM		$22.00		$3.00			
Camisoles	WOM		$26.00		$3.00			
Dresses	B/T		$22.00		$4.00			

← TOTAL FOR PAGE 20

B/T = Baby Toddler

CONTRIBUTION RECORD

For help with valuing your donations, see tips shown on page 78.	Gender	Qty	FMV better (high range)	Qty	FMV good (low range)	Your Total FMV	Estimate Original Purchase Price (Total)	Approx. Year Acquired
Dresses - infant designer (e.g. Burberry)	B/T		$72.00		$22.00			
Dresses - designer (e.g. Oilily, Baby Dior)	B/T		$20.00		$6.00			
Dresses	GIRL		$29.00		$4.00			
Dresses - casual	WOM		$33.00		$3.00			
Dresses - evening	WOM		$60.00		$8.00			
Dresses - career	WOM		$34.00		$5.00			
Pants	B/T		$12.00		$2.00			
Pants - Jeans	CHILD		$21.00		$3.00			
Pants - Jeans	ADULT		$24.00		$8.00			
Pants/Slacks	CHILD		$18.00		$2.00			
Pants/Slacks - casual	WOM		$20.00		$4.00			
Pants/Slacks - casual	MEN		$20.00		$6.00			
Pantsuits - casual	WOM		$43.00		$8.00			

← TOTAL FOR PAGE 21

B/T = Baby Toddler

CLO

CLO

CONTRIBUTION RECORD

For help with valuing your donations, see tips shown on page 78.	Gender	Qty	FMV better (high range)	Qty	FMV good (low range)	Your Total FMV	Estimate Original Purchase Price (Total)	Approx. Year Acquired
Pantsuits - dress/career	WOM		$52.00		$15.00			
Pantsuits - designer (e.g. Prada, Escada, Dolce & Gabbana)	WOM		$140.00		$15.00			
Pants/Slacks - dress/career	WOM		$22.00		$4.00			
Pants/Slacks - dress/career	MEN		$17.00		$3.00			
Pajama/Sleepers	B/T		$13.00		$3.00			
Pajama/Nightgown	GIRL		$24.00		$2.00			
Pajama/Nightgown	WOM		$28.00		$3.00			
Pajamas	BOY		$17.00		$2.00			
Pajamas	MEN		$24.00		$4.00			
Slips - Camisoles	WOM		$26.00		$3.00			
Support/Foundation Undergarment (spandex, girdle)	WOM		$26.00		$4.00			
Scrubs	ADULT		$14.00		$23.00			

← TOTAL FOR PAGE 22

B/T = Baby Toddler

CLO

CONTRIBUTION RECORD

For help with valuing your donations, see tips shown on page 78.	Gender	Qty	FMV better (high range)	Qty	FMV good (low range)	Your Total FMV	Estimate Original Purchase Price (Total)	Approx. Year Acquired
Shirts (Gap/Gymboree)	B/T		$9.00		$3.00			
Shirts-long sleeve	GIRL		$21.00		$3.00			
Shirts - summer/tank	GIRL		$9.00		$1.00			
Shirts	BOY		$12.00		$2.00			
Shirts - summer/tank	BOY		$11.00		$2.00			
Shirt - casual	MEN		$19.00		$4.00			
Shirt - dress	MEN		$22.00		$4.00			
Shirt - golf	MEN		$32.00		$6.00			
Shirt - polo, designer (e.g. Gucci, Polo RL, Louis Vuitton)	MEN		$50.00		$8.00			
Shirt - tuxedo, designer (e.g. Armani, Brioni, Ermenegildo)	MEN		$42.00		$8.00			
Shirt - tank	MEN		$17.00		$3.00			
Shorts	GIRL		$18.00		$4.00			
						← TOTAL FOR PAGE 23		

B/T = Baby Toddler

CONTRIBUTION RECORD

For help with valuing your donations, see tips shown on page 78.	Gender	Qty	FMV better (high range)	Qty	FMV good (low range)	Your Total FMV	Estimate Original Purchase Price (Total)	Approx. Year Acquired
Shorts	BOY		$15.00		$2.00			
Shorts - Capris casual	WOM		$18.00		$3.00			
Shorts (skort) - golf/tennis	WOM		$24.00		$4.00			
Shorts	MEN		$30.00		$3.00			
Skirts	GIRL		$13.00		$3.00			
Skirt - casual	WOM		$20.00		$2.00			
Skirt - dress/career	WOM		$24.00		$4.00			
Skirt - designer (e.g. Burberry, Gucci)	WOM		$80.00		$8.00			
Slacks/Pants - designer (e.g. Gucci, Prada)	WOM		$95.00		$9.00			
Socks ◆	B/T		◆		◆			
Socks ◆	CHILD		◆		◆			
Socks ◆	ADULT		◆		◆			

← **TOTAL FOR PAGE 24**

B/T = Baby Toddler

◆ = Items of minimal monetary value may be donated but are not deductible

CONTRIBUTION RECORD

For help with valuing your donations, see tips shown on page 78.	Gender	Qty	FMV better (high range)	Qty	FMV good (low range)	Your Total FMV	Estimate Original Purchase Price (Total)	Approx. Year Acquired
Sports fan apparel - shirts (non-authentic)	MEN		$16.00		$5.00			
Sports fan apparel - pants	MEN		$28.00		$5.00			
Sports coat	BOY		$32.00		$6.00			
Sports coat - designer (e.g. Brooks Brothers, Ralph Lauren)	BOY		$60.00		$20.00			
Sports coat	MEN		$47.00		$11.00			
Sports coat - cashmere, designer (e.g. Hermès, Ralph Lauren Purple Label, Tom Ford)	MEN		$125.00		$22.00			
Suits	BOY		$62.00		$9.00			
Suits	MEN		$150.00		$15.00			
Suit - tuxedo	BOY		$70.00		$17.00			
Suit - tuxedo	MEN		$125.00		$22.00			
Suits - dress/career	WOM		$67.00		$8.00			
Suits - jogging	WOM		$32.00		$8.00			

← TOTAL FOR PAGE 25

CLO

CLO

CONTRIBUTION RECORD

For help with valuing your donations, see tips shown on page 78.	Gender	Qty	FMV better (high range)	Qty	FMV good (low range)	Your Total FMV	Estimate Original Purchase Price (Total)	Approx. Year Acquired
Sweats (pants or shirts)	CHILD		$15.00		$3.00			
Sweat Shirts	ADULT		$18.00		$4.00			
Sweat Pants	MEN		$28.00		$4.00			
Sweat Pants	WOM		$23.00		$2.00			
Sweaters	CHILD		$14.00		$2.00			
Sweaters long sleeve	WOM		$24.00		$3.00			
Sweaters short sleeve	WOM		$20.00		$4.00			
Sweaters	MEN		$22.00		$6.00			
T-Shirts	B/T		$9.00		$1.00			
T-Shirts	CHILD		$9.00		$1.00			
T-Shirts	WOM		$17.00		$3.00			
T-Shirt	MEN		$19.00		$3.00			
Under shorts - boxers	MEN		$12.00		$4.00			

← **TOTAL FOR PAGE 26**

B/T = Baby Toddler

CONTRIBUTION RECORD

For help with valuing your donations, see tips shown on page 78.	Gender	Qty	FMV better (high range)	Qty	FMV good (low range)	Your Total FMV	Estimate Original Purchase Price (Total)	Approx. Year Acquired
Undershirts - Spanx	MEN		$28.00		$7.00			
Underwear	ALL		$5.00		$3.00			
Vests	CHILD		$9.00		$3.00			
Vests	WOM		$40.00		$5.00			
Vests	MEN		$35.00		$4.00			
Wedding dress (non-designer; use original purchase price to adjust FMV)	WOM		$360.00		$30.00			

Special Note: Items such as infant clothing, socks & underwear may be of minimal value. You can donate them, but no deduction is allowable. If you donate in "lots" (6, 12, etc.) of the same item, you may estimate the FMV and document the deduction for the lot.

← **TOTAL FOR PAGE 27**

CLO

CONTRIBUTION RECORD

For help with valuing your donations, see tips shown on page 78.	Gender	Qty	FMV better (high range)	Qty	FMV good (low range)	Your Total FMV	Estimate Original Purchase Price (Total)	Approx. Year Acquired
OUTERWEAR								
Coats/Jackets	B/T		$32.00		$4.00			
Coats	CHILD		$52.00		$8.00			
Coat - casual/leather	WOM		$185.00		$6.00			
Coat - dress/career	WOM		$85.00		$8.00			
Coat (trench/rain)	MEN		$92.00		$10.00			
Coats (long overcoats) Winter	MEN		$99.00		$20.00			
Coats (long) Leather	MEN		$210.00		$22.00			
Earmuffs, Headbands (winter)	ALL		$15.00		$1.00			
Fedora - designer (e.g. Gucci, Stetson)	MEN		$100.00		$10.00			
Gloves, Scarfs (winter)	ALL		$21.00		$3.00			
Hats	WOM		$28.00		$4.00			

← **TOTAL FOR PAGE 28**

B/T = Baby Toddler

CONTRIBUTION RECORD

For help with valuing your donations, see tips shown on page 78.	Gender	Qty	FMV better (high range)	Qty	FMV good (low range)	Your Total FMV	Estimate Original Purchase Price (Total)	Approx. Year Acquired
Hats - fur	WOM		$65.00		$13.00			
Hats - fur, designer (e.g. Prada)	WOM		$228.00		$25.00			
Hoodies	CHILD		$30.00		$3.00			
Hoodies	ADULT		$45.00		$5.00			
Jacket - outer casual	WOM		$35.00		$5.00			
Jacket - outer winter	WOM		$80.00		$9.00			
Jacket/coat (full length fur)	WOM		$490.00		$21.00			
Jacket/coat (full length leather, faux fur)	WOM		$180.00		$15.00			
Jacket - short leather, faux fur	WOM		$88.00		$8.00			
Jackets - winter	CHILD		$42.00		$10.00			
Jackets - windbreaker	CHILD		$21.00		$7.00			
Jackets - designer (e.g. Burberry, North Face)	CHILD		$68.00		$9.00			
							← TOTAL FOR PAGE 29	OTW

OTW

CONTRIBUTION RECORD

For help with valuing your donations, see tips shown on page 78.	Gender	Qty	FMV better (high range)	Qty	FMV good (low range)	Your Total FMV	Estimate Original Purchase Price (Total)	Approx. Year Acquired
Jackets - short leather	MEN		$120.00		$24.00			
Jackets - winter	MEN		$70.00		$20.00			
Snowsuits	CHILD		$54.00		$6.00			

← TOTAL FOR PAGE 30

CONTRIBUTION RECORD

For help with valuing your donations, see tips shown on page 78.	Gender	Qty	FMV better (high range)	Qty	FMV good (low range)	Your Total FMV	Estimate Original Purchase Price (Total)	Approx. Year Acquired
ACCESSORIES								
Belts - cloth/plastic	CHILD		$7.00		$2.00			
Belts - cloth/plastic	ADULT		$9.00		$3.00			
Belts - leather	CHILD		$15.00		$6.00			
Belts - leather	ADULT		$28.00		$8.00			
Jewelry - costume	WOM		$25.00		$3.00			
Jewelry / watches - casual	MEN		$40.00		$8.00			
Purse / Handbags	WOM		$60.00		$4.00			
Scarves (silk or similar type)	WOM		$42.00		$3.00			
Ties	MEN		$19.00		$2.00			
Umbrella	ADULT		$15.00		$2.00			
Wallets	WOM		$22.00		$5.00			
Wallets	MEN		$20.00		$4.00			
Wigs-Synthetic	WOM		$39.00		$8.00			

← TOTAL FOR PAGE 31

ACC

CONTRIBUTION RECORD

FTW

For help with valuing your donations, see tips shown on page 78.	Gender	Qty	FMV better (high range)	Qty	FMV good (low range)	Your Total FMV	Estimate Original Purchase Price (Total)	Approx. Year Acquired
FOOTWEAR								
Shoes	B/T		$32.00		$5.00			
Shoes - athletic/tennis	CHILD		$40.00		$5.00			
Shoes - athletic/tennis	ADULT		$72.00		$5.00			
Shoes - boots	CHILD		$42.00		$10.00			
Shoes/boots - designer (e.g. UGG, Sorrell, Burberry)	CHILD		$80.00		$16.00			
Shoes - boots	WOM		$110.00		$15.00			
Shoes - boots	MEN		$95.00		$12.00			
Shoes - casual	CHILD		$22.00		$5.00			
Shoes - casual	WOM		$38.00		$5.00			
Shoes - casual, designer (e.g. Louis Vuitton, Prada)	WOM		$70.00		$22.00			
Shoes - casual	MEN		$42.00		$4.00			

← TOTAL FOR PAGE 32

B/T = Baby Toddler

CONTRIBUTION RECORD

For help with valuing your donations, see tips shown on page 78.	Gender	Qty	FMV better (high range)	Qty	FMV good (low range)	Your Total FMV	Estimate Original Purchase Price (Total)	Approx. Year Acquired
Shoes - dress / career	ADULT		$60.00		$7.00			
Shoes - sandal/slipper	CHILD		$14.00		$2.00			
Shoes - sandal/slipper	WOM		$28.00		$3.00			
Shoes - sandal/slipper	MEN		$32.00		$5.00			

← TOTAL FOR PAGE 33

FTW

CONTRIBUTION RECORD

MAT

For help with valuing your donations, see tips shown on page 78.	Gender	Qty	FMV better (high range)	Qty	FMV good (low range)	Your Total FMV	Estimate Original Purchase Price (Total)	Approx. Year Acquired
MATERNITY								
Maternity - bra	WOM		$20.00		$3.00			
Maternity - coat/trench (Mimi, A Pea in the Pod)	WOM		$45.00		$5.00			
Maternity - dress	WOM		$40.00		$3.00			
Maternity - jeans	WOM		$34.00		$5.00			
Maternity - pants/slacks	WOM		$24.00		$4.00			
Maternity - shorts/crop pants	WOM		$18.00		$4.00			
Maternity - skirt	WOM		$20.00		$3.00			
Maternity - support belt (Belly Bandit)	WOM		$35.00		$7.00			
Maternity - support pillow	WOM		$36.00		$6.00			
Maternity - tops long sleeve	WOM		$24.00		$2.00			
Maternity - tops short sleeve	WOM		$14.00		$5.00			

← TOTAL FOR PAGE 34

CONTRIBUTION RECORD

For help with valuing your donations, see tips shown on page 78.	Gender	Qty	FMV better (high range)	Qty	FMV good (low range)	Your Total FMV	Estimate Original Purchase Price (Total)	Approx. Year Acquired
BABY/TODDLER GEAR								
Activity gyms			$24.00		$2.00			
Baby Blocks, toys (Fisher Price, Pottery Barn) (large or set/multiple pieces)			$40.00		$2.00			
Bassinet/cradle			$175.00		$16.00			
Bath seat			$44.00		$5.00			
Bathtub			$26.00		$8.00			
Bibs (6+ regular or single Gymboree)			$6.00		$3.00			
Blankets (quilts/comforters/duvets)			$42.00		$5.00			
Blankets (receiving)			$26.00		$2.00			
Booster seats			$75.00		$20.00			
Bottle warmers			$20.00		$6.00			
Bottles - 6+			$20.00		$3.00			

← TOTAL FOR PAGE 35

BTG

CONTRIBUTION RECORD

For help with valuing your donations, see tips shown on page 78.	Gender	Qty	FMV better (high range)	Qty	FMV good (low range)	Your Total FMV	Estimate Original Purchase Price (Total)	Approx. Year Acquired
Bouncer			$61.00		$10.00			
Boxes/storage/toy chests			$60.00		$23.00			
Breast pumps - Medela, Freestyle, Ameda			$85.00		$20.00			
Breast pumps - other			$42.00		$13.00			
Car seats - convertible			$215.00		$20.00			
Car seats - booster			$48.00		$5.00			
Car seats - high-back booster			$62.00		$15.00			
Carriage			$99.00		$38.00			
Changing pad (contoured/pad)			$35.00		$5.00			
Changing table			$125.00		$15.00			
Crib (portable)			$140.00		$19.00			
Crib (w/mattress)			$150.00		$50.00			
Crib Bumper Pad			$20.00		$13.00			

← TOTAL FOR PAGE 36

CONTRIBUTION RECORD

For help with valuing your donations, see tips shown on page 78.	Gender	Qty	FMV better (high range)	Qty	FMV good (low range)	Your Total FMV	Estimate Original Purchase Price (Total)	Approx. Year Acquired
Crib Mattress			$62.00		$12.00			
Crib Bedding Sets (non-designer bumpers, skirts/dust ruffles, pads, sheets, etc.)			$110.00		$18.00			
Crib Bedding Sets - designer (e.g. Pottery Barn, Cocalo Couture, custom made)			$215.00		$20.00			
Crib sheet sets			$60.00		$5.00			
Crib toys/accessories			$32.00		$12.00			
Diaper bags (non designer)			$12.00		$5.00			
Diaper Genie			$38.00		$10.00			
Dresser			$100.00		$25.00			
High chair			$190.00		$20.00			
Infant baby/toddler backpack (no frame)			$50.00		$10.00			
Infant carrier or sling			$90.00		$4.00			
Jumpers (doorway)			$35.00		$10.00			

← TOTAL FOR PAGE 37

BTG

CONTRIBUTION RECORD

For help with valuing your donations, see tips shown on page 78.	Gender	Qty	FMV better (high range)	Qty	FMV good (low range)	Your Total FMV	Estimate Original Purchase Price (Total)	Approx. Year Acquired
Jumpers/exerciser - designer (Baby Einstein, FP)			$62.00		$12.00			
Mobiles			$50.00		$12.00			
Monitors (Fisher-Price, Graco - no video)			$45.00		$20.00			
Nursery lamps			$30.00		$5.00			
Playpen			$99.00		$7.00			
Potty chair			$70.00		$11.00			
Rattles & teethers (large toy style or 4+ small)			$19.00		$4.00			
Rocking chair/gliders			$120.00		$70.00			
Safety gates			$60.00		$5.00			
Stroller - double			$390.00		$40.00			
Stroller - folding			$95.00		$34.00			
Stroller - single			$320.00		$7.00			

← TOTAL FOR PAGE 38

BTG

CONTRIBUTION RECORD

For help with valuing your donations, see tips shown on page 78.	Gender	Qty	FMV better (high range)	Qty	FMV good (low range)	Your Total FMV	Estimate Original Purchase Price (Total)	Approx. Year Acquired
Stroller/Jogger - designer (e.g. 4Moms, City Select, Phil & Teds)			$430.00		$75.00			
Swing			$170.00		$20.00			
Toddler bed			$190.00		$22.00			
Towels - bath/washcloth sets			$7.00		$1.00			
Walkers/saucers			$52.00		$20.00			
Wall décor			$68.00		$5.00			

← TOTAL FOR PAGE 39

BTG

CONTRIBUTION RECORD

For help with valuing your donations, see tips shown on page 78.	Gender	Qty	FMV better (high range)	Qty	FMV good (low range)	Your Total FMV	Estimate Original Purchase Price (Total)	Approx. Year Acquired
CRAFTS								
Completed projects, used instruction books (e.g. crochet, cross-stitch)			$25.00		$4.00			
Handmade afghans			$45.00		$5.00			
Handmade quilts baby			$48.00		$7.00			
Handmade quilts/samplers bed size			$36.00		$3.00			
Kits (to make)			$30.00		$2.00			
Sewing Machine (beginner)			$109.00		$30.00			
Supplies, yarn, fabric, beads, notions (multiple pieces)			$20.00		$3.00			

← TOTAL FOR PAGE 40

CONTRIBUTION RECORD

For help with valuing your donations, see tips shown on page 78.	Gender	Qty	FMV better (high range)	Qty	FMV good (low range)	Your Total FMV	Estimate Original Purchase Price (Total)	Approx. Year Acquired
DRY GOODS								
Bedspreads/quilts			$116.00		$12.00			
Blankets			$45.00		$7.00			
Blankets - electric			$57.00		$20.00			
Chair/sofa covers			$34.00		$14.00			
Chair seat pads			$40.00		$8.00			
Dust Ruffles			$32.00		$9.00			
Mattress pad			$56.00		$2.00			
Mattress topper			$140.00		$10.00			
Pillows - bed			$25.00		$12.00			
Pillows - décor			$23.00		$10.00			
Pillows - memory foam			$70.00		$8.00			
Place mats - set of 4+			$35.00		$4.00			

← TOTAL FOR PAGE 41

DRY

CONTRIBUTION RECORD

DRY

For help with valuing your donations, see tips shown on page 78.	Gender	Qty	FMV better (high range)	Qty	FMV good (low range)	Your Total FMV	Estimate Original Purchase Price (Total)	Approx. Year Acquired
Rugs - throw			$52.00		$7.00			
Rugs - room size			$420.00		$45.00			
Shams - set			$42.00		$8.00			
Sheets - full (each)			$26.00		$5.00			
Sheets - queen/king (each)			$46.00		$10.00			
Sheets - twin (each)			$18.00		$5.00			
Shower curtain			$37.00		$4.00			
Tablecloth			$23.00		$2.00			
Throws (fleece)			$23.00		$5.00			
Towels - bath			$24.00		$9.00			
Towels - guest			$12.00		$3.00			
Towels - hand			$12.00		$3.00			
Towels - kitchen			$9.00		$3.00			

← TOTAL FOR PAGE 42

CONTRIBUTION RECORD

For help with valuing your donations, see tips shown on page 78.	Gender	Qty	FMV better (high range)	Qty	FMV good (low range)	Your Total FMV	Estimate Original Purchase Price (Total)	Approx. Year Acquired
Window cover - Curtains			$18.00		$3.00			
Window cover - Drapes			$60.00		$9.00			
Window cover - Horizontal or Vertical Blinds - most charities will not accept, call first!			$58.00		$8.00			

← TOTAL FOR PAGE 43

DRY

CONTRIBUTION RECORD

DEC

For help with valuing your donations, see tips shown on page 78.	Gender	Qty	FMV better (high range)	Qty	FMV good (low range)	Your Total FMV	Estimate Original Purchase Price (Total)	Approx. Year Acquired
DÉCOR								
Art Glass/pottery			$25.00		$5.00			
Baskets (large)			$32.00		$4.00			
Baskets (medium-small)			$18.00		$5.00			
Bathroom soap dish			$15.00		$7.00			
Bathroom toothbrush holder			$11.00		$6.00			
Bathroom tissue box holder			$22.00		$5.00			
Fireplace tool set (solid brass)			$310.00		$20.00			
Fireplace tool set (plated)			$50.00		$7.00			
Frames (photo)			$20.00		$2.00			
Halloween decor/costumes			$50.00		$3.00			
Holiday Christmas tree (6')			$140.00		$19.00			
Holiday décor			$30.00		$4.00			

← TOTAL FOR PAGE 44

CONTRIBUTION RECORD

For help with valuing your donations, see tips shown on page 78.	Gender	Qty	FMV better (high range)	Qty	FMV good (low range)	Your Total FMV	Estimate Original Purchase Price (Total)	Approx. Year Acquired
Knick Knacks / Chachkees					$3.00			
Picture/Painting - framed large			$110.00		$15.00			
Picture/Painting - framed small/medium			$58.00		$5.00			
Sculpture/large figurines			$30.00		$5.00			
Silk (artificial) plant - 6"			$28.00		$7.00			
Vase			$32.00		$5.00			

← TOTAL FOR PAGE 45

DEC

CONTRIBUTION RECORD

ELE

For help with valuing your donations, see tips shown on page 78.	Gender	Qty	FMV better (high range)	Qty	FMV good (low range)	Your Total FMV	Estimate Original Purchase Price (Total)	Approx. Year Acquired
ELECTRONICS - ALL WORKING CONDITION								
Adding machine (desk with paper roll)			$42.00		$4.00			
Bathroom scale			$29.00		$5.00			
Calculator (TI Business/Graphing)			$90.00		$12.00			
Cameras - (digital, small/compact, few features)			$35.00		$15.00			
Cameras - plastic (older, disposable)			$16.00		$3.00			
CD Player (portable)			$40.00		$10.00			
CD Player / Boombox			$60.00		$15.00			
Cell phone (basic flip-phone)			$50.00		$5.00			
Cell phone (newer smartphones)			$490.00		$90.00			
Cell phone (older smartphones)			$270.00		$20.00			
Cell phone other newer			$52.00		$10.00			

← TOTAL FOR PAGE 46

CONTRIBUTION RECORD

For help with valuing your donations, see tips shown on page 78.	Gender	Qty	FMV better (high range)	Qty	FMV good (low range)	Your Total FMV	Estimate Original Purchase Price (Total)	Approx. Year Acquired
Clock - alarm			$27.00		$5.00			
Clock - alarm (Bose)			$380.00		$75.00			
Clock - radio w/alarm			$35.00		$5.00			
Clock - for iPod (iHome/similar)			$40.00		$3.00			
Clock - wall			$45.00		$5.00			
Copier (office style - check with charity if they accept)			$350.00		$80.00			
DVD Players / Recorders (older)			$90.00		$10.00			
Home Theatres - sound system (surround)			$225.00		$40.00			
iPod (3rd/4th Gen)			$80.00		$20.00			
iPod (mini)			$40.00		$10.00			
Navigation System (GPS - older models)			$90.00		$13.00			
PDA (older models)			$80.00		$5.00			

ELE

← TOTAL FOR PAGE 47

CONTRIBUTION RECORD

ELE

For help with valuing your donations, see tips shown on page 78.	Gender	Qty	FMV better (high range)	Qty	FMV good (low range)	Your Total FMV	Estimate Original Purchase Price (Total)	Approx. Year Acquired
Radio (transistor/other)			$450.00		8.00			
Shortwave Radios			$170.00		29.00			
Stereo (radio, cassette/turntable, CD combo)			$70.00		20.00			
Stereo Receiver - components (e.g. Sherwood, Kenwood)			$90.00		45.00			
Telephone - answering machine			$45.00		5.00			
Telephone - desk/rotary/corded/vintage			$55.00		7.00			
Telephone - digital home style cordless - single phone			$45.00		9.00			
NOTE: Before donating televisions check with your charity to make sure they are accepted.								
Television - small - older			$25.00		$15.00			
Television - medium - older			$40.00		$18.00			
Television - large - older			$60.00		$20.00			

← TOTAL FOR PAGE 48

CONTRIBUTION RECORD

For help with valuing your donations, see tips shown on page 78.	Gender	Qty	FMV better (high range)	Qty	FMV good (low range)	Your Total FMV	Estimate Original Purchase Price (Total)	Approx. Year Acquired
Television - flat screen 19"-27"			$119.00		$20.00			
Television - flat screen 32" or larger			$250.00		$40.00			
Tivo (receiver only)			$135.00		$25.00			
Typewriter (home models)			$60.00		$16.00			
VCR (older model)			$40.00		$10.00			
Video handheld camcorder (older model, non-digital)			$65.00		$20.00			

See COM - computers, peripherals for printers, scanners, etc.

← TOTAL FOR PAGE 49

ELE

CONTRIBUTION RECORD

ENT

For help with valuing your donations, see tips shown on page 78.	Gender	Qty	FMV better (high range)	Qty	FMV good (low range)	Your Total FMV	Estimate Original Purchase Price (Total)	Approx. Year Acquired
ENTERTAINMENT								
AudioBooks - CD or Cassette			$22.00		$3.00			
Books - children/youth hardcover			$20.00		$3.00			
Books - children/youth paperback			$5.00		$1.00			
Books - coffee table			$32.00		$3.00			
Books - hardcover			$22.00		$4.00			
Books - paperback (each)			$6.00		$2.00			
Books - text (usable)			$80.00		$5.00			
DVD - movies			$18.00		$2.00			
DVD - movies Disney / new release			$26.00		$2.00			
Music (CD or Cassette)			$14.00		$2.00			
Records/albums			$20.00		$1.00			
VHS Videos			$10.00		$3.00			

Special Note: Books (non vintage) and media tapes are of minimal monetary value. If you donate in quantity (6, 12, etc.) of the same item, please estimate a FMV for all. If you only have 1 or 2 = give it to the charity, but you cannot take a deduction

← **TOTAL FOR PAGE 50**

CONTRIBUTION RECORD

For help with valuing your donations, see tips shown on page 78.	Gender	Qty	FMV better (high range)	Qty	FMV good (low range)	Your Total FMV	Estimate Original Purchase Price (Total)	Approx. Year Acquired
GARDEN/LAWN								
BBQ grill			$140.00		$25.00			
Ladder/2-3 step			$50.00		$17.00			
Leaf blower (handheld)			$120.00		$25.00			
Mower garden/lawn - riding 💰			$1,400.00		$200.00			
Mower - walking/push			$320.00		$30.00			
Power Edger / Weedwacker			$80.00		$25.00			
Rototiller (garden)			$250.00		$125.00			
Shop vacuum			$160.00		$15.00			
Snow blower/thrower			$475.00		$150.00			
Tools - garden/hand			$11.00		$4.00			
Tools - large/garden			$22.00		$5.00			

← TOTAL FOR PAGE 51

💰 = Qualified Appraisal Required.

GAR

CONTRIBUTION RECORD

KIT

For help with valuing your donations, see tips shown on page 78.	Gender	Qty	FMV better (high range)	Qty	FMV good (low range)	Your Total FMV	Estimate Original Purchase Price (Total)	Approx. Year Acquired
KITCHEN								
Baking pans/bakeware			$40.00		$4.00			
Blender (older Kitchenaid, Oster)			$52.00		$15.00			
Bread machine			$120.00		$15.00			
Cake pan (e.g. Wilton, shaped)			$30.00		$3.00			
Can opener - electric			$49.00		$5.00			
Casserole dish (Pyrex)			$25.00		$5.00			
Coffeemaker - drip			$50.00		$5.00			
Coffeemaker - percolator			$40.00		$5.00			
Coffeemaker - Keurig			$100.00		$20.00			
Coffeemaker - single serve pod (Black & Decker, Philips)			$70.00		$15.00			
Dish/Plate - casual china			$14.00		$3.00			

← TOTAL FOR PAGE 52

CONTRIBUTION RECORD

For help with valuing your donations, see tips shown on page 78.	Gender	Qty	FMV better (high range)	Qty	FMV good (low range)	Your Total FMV	Estimate Original Purchase Price (Total)	Approx. Year Acquired
Dish/Plate - fine china			$25.00		$15.00			
Dish/Plate - plastic 4+			$15.00		$8.00			
Dish set - complete service (e.g. Melamine, Gibson)			$70.00		$25.00			
Dish set - service for 4 (e.g. Pfaltzgraff, fine china)			$150.00		$13.00			
Food processor (countertop model)			$65.00		$22.00			
Food storage (plastic)			$45.00		$3.00			
Gadgets/Utensils - kitchen			$12.00		$2.00			
Glasses/mugs (ea)			$8.00		$1.00			
Grills (George Foreman)			$40.00		$8.00			
Juicer - electric (Juiceman, Jack LaLanne)			$70.00		$7.00			
Microwave oven (countertop)			$80.00		$20.00			
Mixer - electric hand			$40.00		$5.00			
							← TOTAL FOR PAGE 53	

KIT

CONTRIBUTION RECORD

KIT

For help with valuing your donations, see tips shown on page 78.	Gender	Qty	FMV better (high range)	Qty	FMV good (low range)	Your Total FMV	Estimate Original Purchase Price (Total)	Approx. Year Acquired
Mixer - stand (Hamilton Beach, Drink-Master)			$55.00		$10.00			
Mixer - stand (e.g. Kitchenaid nonprofessional)			$180.00		$39.00			
Pampered Chef baking/cookware			$41.00		$5.00			
Pie Plates (Pyrex)			$15.00		$3.00			
Potholder/Ovenmit (fabric/silicone)			$25.00		$3.00			
Potholder (trivet)			$12.00		$3.00			
Pots/pans			$40.00		$10.00			
Salt & Pepper shaker			$9.00		$1.00			
Salt & Pepper shaker (e.g. Vintage, Lenox)			$23.00		$2.00			
Serving dishes/platters			$45.00		$5.00			
Skillet/Griddle - electric			$75.00		$8.00			

← **TOTAL FOR PAGE 54**

CONTRIBUTION RECORD

For help with valuing your donations, see tips shown on page 78.	Gender	Qty	FMV better (high range)	Qty	FMV good (low range)	Your Total FMV	Estimate Original Purchase Price (Total)	Approx. Year Acquired
Slow Cooker (e.g. Crock-Pot)			$36.00		$5.00			
Toaster - 2 slice			$25.00		$12.00			
Toaster/broiler oven			$58.00		$12.00			
Utensils - BBQ set (4+ pieces)			$28.00		$11.00			
Utensils - carving set			$58.00		$15.00			
Utensils - everyday flatware each piece			$6.00		$1.00			

← TOTAL FOR PAGE 55

KIT

CONTRIBUTION RECORD

LUG

For help with valuing your donations, see tips shown on page 78.	Gender	Qty	FMV better (high range)	Qty	FMV good (low range)	Your Total FMV	Estimate Original Purchase Price (Total)	Approx. Year Acquired
LUGGAGE								
Briefcase (Leather)			$93.00		$13.00			
Briefcase/Laptop Case (fabric)			$62.00		$9.00			
Carry-on			$68.00		$17.00			
Garment bag - hanging			$42.00		$10.00			
Suitcase - roller			$70.00		$10.00			
Suitcase - standard (no wheels)			$25.00		$5.00			
Trunk			$140.00		$10.00			

← TOTAL FOR PAGE 56

CONTRIBUTION RECORD

For help with valuing your donations, see tips shown on page 78.	Gender	Qty	FMV better (high range)	Qty	FMV good (low range)	Your Total FMV	Estimate Original Purchase Price (Total)	Approx. Year Acquired
MUSICAL INSTRUMENTS								
Brass (coronet, horn, trumpet, french horn student band)			$200.00		$85.00			
Guitar - acoustic 💲			$1,600.00		$350.00			
Guitar - beginner/starter			$100.00		$15.00			
Guitar - electric			$258.00		$30.00			
Harmonica			$60.00		$10.00			
Keyboard -smaller versions (e.g. Casio)			$200.00		$28.00			
Organ (console)			$225.00		$49.00			
Percussion (drum set) 💲			$2,700.00		$111.00			
Percussion (drum, snare student band)			$70.00		$19.00			
Piano - upright 💲			$1,220.00		$65.00			

← **TOTAL FOR PAGE 57**

💲 = Qualified Appraisal Required.

MUS

CONTRIBUTION RECORD

MUS

For help with valuing your donations, see tips shown on page 78.	Gender	Qty	FMV better (high range)	Qty	FMV good (low range)	Your Total FMV	Estimate Original Purchase Price (Total)	Approx. Year Acquired
Violin - student			$290.00		$10.00			
Woodwind clarinet (student band/beginner)			$80.00		$60.00			
Woodwind (clarinet – Yamaha) 💰			$670.00		$450.00			
Woodwind flute (e.g. Jupiter)			$480.00		$90.00			
Woodwind flute (student band)			$80.00		$60.00			

💰 = Qualified Appraisal Required.

← TOTAL FOR PAGE 58

CONTRIBUTION RECORD

For help with valuing your donations, see tips shown on page 78.	Gender	Qty	FMV better (high range)	Qty	FMV good (low range)	Your Total FMV	Estimate Original Purchase Price (Total)	Approx. Year Acquired
PETS								
Bedding			$53.00		$6.00			
Cat climbing condo - small			$53.00		$6.00			
Crates/carriers metal			$101.00		$10.00			
Crates/carriers molded plastic or fabric with or without rollers			$80.00		$13.00			
Litter box - automatic			$290.00		$46.00			
Litter box - standard/covered			$42.00		$12.00			
Pet dish - automatic			$31.00		$5.00			
Pet dish - standard			$30.00		$4.00			
Pet toys (Kong, FroliCat)			$16.00		$3.00			

← TOTAL FOR PAGE 59

PET

CONTRIBUTION RECORD

For help with valuing your donations, see tips shown on page 78.	Gender	Qty	FMV better (high range)	Qty	FMV good (low range)	Your Total FMV	Estimate Original Purchase Price (Total)	Approx. Year Acquired
WORKSHOP								
Battery charger (auto, trickle charge)			$24.00		$16.00			
Battery tester - non-digital			$90.00		$4.00			
Circular saw			$160.00		$15.00			
Cordless nail gun (e.g. Paslode, Ramset)			$270.00		$56.00			
Cordless drill (e.g. Craftsman, B&D; DeWalt)			$115.00		$10.00			
Cordless screwdriver - handheld small (e.g. Black & Decker)			$22.00		$8.00			
Hand tools (hammer, screwdriver, etc.)			$24.00		$4.00			
Sander (handheld belt, variable speed Black & Decker)			$140.00		$24.00			
Tablesaw - on stand (Craftsman, Ryobi)			$170.00		$60.00			
Wrench - heavy duty (pipe)			$95.00		$5.00			

← TOTAL FOR PAGE 60

CONTRIBUTION RECORD

For help with valuing your donations, see tips shown on page 78.	Gender	Qty	FMV better (high range)	Qty	FMV good (low range)	Your Total FMV	Estimate Original Purchase Price (Total)	Approx. Year Acquired
SPORTS & EXERCISE								
Ab Lounger (older)			$90.00		$40.00			
Abdominal exercisers (twist, ab roller, wheels)			$90.00		$7.00			
Backpack - hiking (internal/external frame)			$110.00		$17.00			
Backpack - standard (student)			$38.00		$8.00			
Baseball bat - youth			$215.00		$14.00			
Baseball glove			$60.00		$11.00			
Basketball, football, soccer ball			$40.00		$7.00			
Bicycle - common (e.g. Huffy)			$210.00		$30.00			
Bicycle - specialty* 💰 (e.g. Bianchi)			$1,099.00		$225.00			
Bicycle - child			$180.00		$12.00			

💰 = Qualified Appraisal Required.

← TOTAL FOR PAGE 61

S&E

CONTRIBUTION RECORD

S&E

For help with valuing your donations, see tips shown on page 78.	Gender	Qty	FMV better (high range)	Qty	FMV good (low range)	Your Total FMV	Estimate Original Purchase Price (Total)	Approx. Year Acquired
Bicycle - helmet			$45.00		$5.00			
Bowling ball			$40.00		$25.00			
Bowling ball* (e.g. Ebonite, Hammer, Lane)			$90.00		$11.00			
Bowling shoes			$60.00		$10.00			
Boxing gloves			$70.00		$8.00			
Camping - sleeping bag (non camping kids character print)			$40.00		$7.00			
Camping - sleeping bag			$200.00		$15.00			
Camping - tent			$220.00		$21.00			
Canoes (Old Town) 💰			$3,300.00		$50.00			
Dumbbells - hand (individual)			$40.00		$5.00			
Elliptical machine (smaller in-home)			$320.00		$39.00			

← TOTAL FOR PAGE 62

*Quality and models vary dramatically based on original purchase price.
💰 = Qualified Appraisal Required.

CONTRIBUTION RECORD

For help with valuing your donations, see tips shown on page 78.	Gender	Qty	FMV better (high range)	Qty	FMV good (low range)	Your Total FMV	Estimate Original Purchase Price (Total)	Approx. Year Acquired
Exercise bike			$370.00		$50.00			
Fishing pole (bamboo)			$40.00		$21.00			
Fishing reel			$42.00		$7.00			
Fishing Rod (non fly)			$150.00		$23.00			
Football helmet - adult			$290.00		$30.00			
Football helmet - youth			$90.00		$12.00			
Golf bag			$175.00		$15.00			
Golf club - single			$90.00		$9.00			
Golf clubs (beginner or older sets)			$92.00		$38.00			
Inversion table			$320.00		$50.00			
Kayaks - lower end models			$475.00		$150.00			
Pilates (DVD/gear)			$20.00		$1.00			

← TOTAL FOR PAGE 63

S&E

CONTRIBUTION RECORD

S&E

For help with valuing your donations, see tips shown on page 78.	Gender	Qty	FMV better (high range)	Qty	FMV good (low range)	Your Total FMV	Estimate Original Purchase Price (Total)	Approx. Year Acquired
Ping Pong table			$450.00		$40.00			
Pool table (with balls, rack, cues)			$490.00		$175.00			
Skateboard			$110.00		$15.00			
Skates - ice			$78.00		$10.00			
Skates - roller (older style)			$130.00		$10.00			
Skates - in-line			$78.00		$7.00			
Ski Machine - wood - (e.g. Nordic Track)			$369.00		$50.00			
Skis (snow, blades, water)			$320.00		$40.00			
Sled			$80.00		$15.00			
Soccer shoes			$42.00		$7.00			
Softballs (each)			$3.00		$1.00			
Steps & Blocks			$80.00		$10.00			

← TOTAL FOR PAGE 64

CONTRIBUTION RECORD

For help with valuing your donations, see tips shown on page 78.	Gender	Qty	FMV better (high range)	Qty	FMV good (low range)	Your Total FMV	Estimate Original Purchase Price (Total)	Approx. Year Acquired
Tennis/Squash racquet			$52.00		$10.00			
Thigh exercisers			$36.00		$5.00			
Toboggan			$150.00		$40.00			
Weight bench w/weights (home set)			$200.00		$30.00			
Yoga/exercise mats			$45.00		$6.00			

← TOTAL FOR PAGE 65

S&E

CONTRIBUTION RECORD

TOY

For help with valuing your donations, see tips shown on page 78.	Gender	Qty	FMV better (high range)	Qty	FMV good (low range)	Your Total FMV	Estimate Original Purchase Price (Total)	Approx. Year Acquired
TOYS								
Action figures (noncollectible)			$15.00		$3.00			
Beanie Babies (non rare)			$20.00		$3.00			
Board games			$20.00		$7.00			
Die-cast cars (e.g. Matchbox, Hot Wheels noncollectible, multiple pieces)			$15.00		$2.00			
Die-cast models			$65.00		$6.00			
Dolls - (e.g. Barbie, baby)			$85.00		$10.00			
Fast-food/cereal premiums (multiple 10+)			$21.00		$2.00			
Puzzles - jigsaw			$20.00		$1.00			
Radio control toy vehicles			$65.00		$12.00			
Rocking horse (plush, plastic)			$190.00		$40.00			
Stuffed animals			$30.00		$1.00			

← TOTAL FOR PAGE 66

Vintage toys, stuffed animals and trading cards are in-demand. Research on eBay or other auction site for fair market value.

CONTRIBUTION RECORD

For help with valuing your donations, see tips shown on page 78.	Gender	Qty	FMV better (high range)	Qty	FMV good (low range)	Your Total FMV	Estimate Original Purchase Price (Total)	Approx. Year Acquired
VIDEO GAMES/SYSTEMS - ALL WORKING CONDITION								
Atari (2600 system with games)			$250.00		$70.00			
Games for video game systems			$65.00		$4.00			
Leapster system (Leapfrog with games/charger)			$26.00		$13.00			
Nintendo 64 system (with games)			$330.00		$40.00			
Nintendo DS (original/Lite)			$80.00		$20.00			
Nintendo DS games			$70.00		$10.00			
Nintendo Game Boy (original)			$85.00		$11.00			
Nintendo Game Boy Advance SP			$95.00		$20.00			
Nintendo Gamecube (system with games)			$99.00		$20.00			
Nintendo NES system (with games)			$200.00		$40.00			
Nintendo Wii			$125.00		$22.00			

← TOTAL FOR PAGE 67

Vintage systems and games are in-demand. Research on eBay or other auction site for fair market value.

VGS

CONTRIBUTION RECORD

VGS

For help with valuing your donations, see tips shown on page 78.	Gender	Qty	FMV better (high range)	Qty	FMV good (low range)	Your Total FMV	Estimate Original Purchase Price (Total)	Approx. Year Acquired
Nintendo Wii Remote (each)			$25.00		$15.00			
Sega Dreamcast system (with games)			$140.00		$50.00			
Sega Genesis system (with games)			$90.00		$11.00			
Sony Playstation system (with games)			$70.00		$10.00			
Sony PS2 (with games)			$90.00		$30.00			
Sony PSP system (with games)			$145.00		$32.00			
Video game controller			$96.00		$7.00			
Vtech Vsmile Pocket			$24.00		$10.00			
Xbox (original with games)			$180.00		$25.00			
Xbox 360 (Arcade with games)			$220.00		$23.00			

| Vintage systems and games are in-demand. Research on eBay or other auction site for fair market value. | | | | | | ← **TOTAL FOR PAGE 68** | |

CONTRIBUTION RECORD

For help with valuing your donations, see tips shown on page 78.	Gender	Qty	FMV better (high range)	Qty	FMV good (low range)	Your Total FMV	Estimate Original Purchase Price (Total)	Approx. Year Acquired
FURNITURE								
Armoire/closet/wardrobe			$390.00		$20.00			
Bar Stools			$80.00		$35.00			
Bed (headboard & frame- full/king/queen)			$200.00		$100.00			
Bed (complete - single)			$150.00		$40.00			
Bedroom set - child			$250.00		$65.00			
Bedroom set - complete 💰			$1,200.00		$150.00			
Bookcase large/tall			$129.00		$30.00			
Bookcase small			$71.00		$10.00			
Ceiling fan			$55.00		$25.00			
Chair - kitchen, wood			$42.00		$15.00			
Chair - office			$100.00		$30.00			
Chair - recliner			$125.00		$25.00			

← TOTAL FOR PAGE 69

💰 = Qualified Appraisal Required.

F&M

CONTRIBUTION RECORD

F&M

For help with valuing your donations, see tips shown on page 78.	Gender	Qty	FMV better (high range)	Qty	FMV good (low range)	Your Total FMV	Estimate Original Purchase Price (Total)	Approx. Year Acquired
Chair - rocking			$90.00		$15.00			
Chair - upholstered			$170.00		$35.00			
Chair - waiting room			$25.00		$5.00			
Chest of Drawers			$150.00		$10.00			
China Cabinet			$250.00		$50.00			
Coffee table			$100.00		$10.00			
Cot (army/camping)			$50.00		$10.00			
Desk (office, Steelcase)			$200.00		$25.00			
Desk - small/student			$40.00		$5.00			
Dining room set (complete) 💰			$1,400.00		$175.00			
Dresser w/mirror			$239.00		$30.00			
End table (each)			$99.00		$20.00			
Folding beds			$70.00		$20.00			
						← TOTAL FOR PAGE 70		

💰 = Qualified Appraisal Required.

CONTRIBUTION RECORD

For help with valuing your donations, see tips shown on page 78.	Gender	Qty	FMV better (high range)	Qty	FMV good (low range)	Your Total FMV	Estimate Original Purchase Price (Total)	Approx. Year Acquired
Futon - (with mattress)			$170.00		$25.00			
Hi Riser (trundle/daybed)			$150.00		$30.00			
Kitchen cabinets/island			$490.00		$50.00			
Kitchen table			$265.00		$35.00			
Kitchen/dinette set			$480.00		$70.00			
Lamp - floor			$90.00		$10.00			
Lamp - table			$110.00		$16.00			
Lighting - chandeliers			$180.00		$15.00			
Lighting - light fixtures			$35.00		$5.00			
Mannequin/dressform			$110.00		$40.00			
Mattress (single) new/like new*			$130.00		$60.00			
Mattress Foundation (single) - new/like new*			$90.00		$40.00			
Mattress (full/dbl) new/like new*			$400.00		$90.00			

← TOTAL FOR PAGE 71

Mattress - *Verify your charity will take anything other than new.

F&M

CONTRIBUTION RECORD

F&M

For help with valuing your donations, see tips shown on page 78.	Gender	Qty	FMV better (high range)	Qty	FMV good (low range)	Your Total FMV	Estimate Original Purchase Price (Total)	Approx. Year Acquired
Mattress Foundation (full/dbl) - new/like new*			$85.00		$35.00			
Mattress (queen/king) - new/like new*			$490.00		$120.00			
Mattress Foundation (queen/king) - new/like new*			$145.00		$58.00			
Sideboard (buffet/cabinet)			$495.00		$90.00			
Secretary			$300.00		$70.00			
Sofa / couch / loveseat			$400.00		$50.00			
Sofa Sleeper (with mattress)			$200.00		$60.00			
TV/Entertainment center			$440.00		$23.00			
TV Stand			$170.00		$14.00			

← **TOTAL FOR PAGE 72**

Mattress - *Verify your charity will take anything other than new.

CONTRIBUTION RECORD

For help with valuing your donations, see tips shown on page 78.	Gender	Qty	FMV better (high range)	Qty	FMV good (low range)	Your Total FMV	Estimate Original Purchase Price (Total)	Approx. Year Acquired
MEDICAL								
Bed - medical			$325.00		$50.00			
Boot cast - walking			$35.00		$11.00			
Cane			$40.00		$10.00			
Crutches - forearm			$150.00		$26.00			
Crutches - wood/aluminum			$80.00		$5.00			
Shower chair			$80.00		$12.00			
Shower transfer bench			$150.00		$15.00			
Toilet seat riser			$35.00		$13.00			
Walker - hospital issue			$40.00		$19.00			
Wheelchair - transport/older			$160.00		$25.00			

← TOTAL FOR PAGE 73

F&M

CONTRIBUTION RECORD

For help with valuing your donations, see tips shown on page 78.	Gender	Qty	FMV better (high range)	Qty	FMV good (low range)	Your Total FMV	Estimate Original Purchase Price (Total)	Approx. Year Acquired
APPLIANCES - ALL WORKING CONDITION								
Air Conditioner - room			$298.00		$42.00			
Dehumidifier			$160.00		$46.00			
Dryer (clothes)			$160.00		$75.00			
Fan - large			$80.00		$11.00			
Fan - small			$25.00		$6.00			
Freezer (chest)			$330.00		$40.00			
Hair dryer / curling / flat iron (handheld)			$50.00		$9.00			
Heaters (space)			$40.00		$19.00			
Iron (clothes)			$45.00		$3.00			
Refrigerator 💰			$3,300.00		$100.00			
Roomba (older model)			$210.00		$30.00			
Stove/oven/range - Electric			$130.00		$55.00			

← TOTAL FOR PAGE 74

💰 = Qualified Appraisal Required.

CONTRIBUTION RECORD

For help with valuing your donations, see tips shown on page 78.	Gender	Qty	FMV better (high range)	Qty	FMV good (low range)	Your Total FMV	Estimate Original Purchase Price (Total)	Approx. Year Acquired
Stove/oven/range - Gas			$250.00		$125.00			
Vacuum - small handheld			$60.00		$8.00			
Vacuum cleaner (common department store variety)			$99.00		$35.00			
Vaporizer - room (common drug store variety)			$45.00		$7.00			
Washing machine			$230.00		$55.00			

← TOTAL FOR PAGE 75

APP

CONTRIBUTION RECORD

For help with valuing your donations, see tips shown on page 78.	Gender	Qty	FMV better (high range)	Qty	FMV good (low range)	Your Total FMV	Estimate Original Purchase Price (Total)	Approx. Year Acquired
COMPUTER AND PERIPHERALS - ALL WORKING CONDITION — Verify your charity accepts computer equipment!								
Apple Powerbook Laptop - G3			$150.00		$35.00			
Apple desktop - G4			$250.00		$33.00			
Apple IIc/SE			$495.00		$50.00			
Desktop PC (bundle) - newer			$480.00		$40.00			
Desktop PC (tower only) older 3yrs+			$300.00		$25.00			
Keyboards (desktop, wired, non-gaming)			$40.00		$9.00			
Laptops / Notebooks older 3yrs+ (HP, NEC)			$275.00		$80.00			
Monitors - Flat screen			$80.00		$10.00			
Monitors - older (CRT)			$50.00		$5.00			
Printer (All-in-one, older home model/ larger HP)			$188.00		$10.00			

← TOTAL FOR PAGE 76

COM

CONTRIBUTION RECORD

For help with valuing your donations, see tips shown on page 78.	Gender	Qty	FMV better (high range)	Qty	FMV good (low range)	Your Total FMV	Estimate Original Purchase Price (Total)	Approx. Year Acquired
Printers - deskjet, small laser (e.g. HP, Cannon, Epson)			$152.00		$35.00			
Projectors - LCD (older)			$400.00		$25.00			
Scanners (one page flatbed)			$65.00		$20.00			
Software (educational, learning, etc.)			$32.00		$5.00			
Speakers (single piece or small 2 piece set)			$20.00		$5.00			

← TOTAL FOR PAGE 77

COM

CONTRIBUTION RECORD

For help with valuing your donations, see tips shown on page 78.	Gender	Qty	FMV better (high range)	Qty	FMV good (low range)	Your Total FMV	Estimate Original Purchase Price (Total)	Approx. Year Acquired

DESIGNER ITEMS

Designer items have a higher fair market value (FMV) than typical or everyday articles of clothing or household goods. Name-brand and designer clothing must have the sewn-in label intact. The final list called "Your Page" in the Contribution Record section includes blank lines for you to describe and value designer items. Please note that qualified appraisals are necessary for single items over $500.

ITEMS NOT LISTED, COLLECTIBLES AND ANTIQUES

These items are unique, and it is appropriate to value them individually. The final list called "Your Page" in the Contribution Record section includes blank lines for you to describe and value items not listed in Deduct It! Deduct It!, collectibles and antiques. Keep in mind that the FMV of these items may be determined by:

- Searching similar items on eBay using filters 'Completed Listings' and 'Sold Items'.
- Searching craigslist.org, or other auction sites
- Similar items at local thrift, resale shops or garage sales
- Catalogs for collectibles
- Qualified appraisals (necessary for single items over $500 or items/groups of similar items over $5,000)

← TOTAL FOR PAGE 78

CONTRIBUTION RECORD

For help with valuing your donations, see tips shown on page 78.	Gender	Qty	FMV better (high range)	Qty	FMV good (low range)	Your Total FMV	Estimate Original Purchase Price (Total)	Approx. Year Acquired
YOUR PAGE — TO DETERMINE FMV, RESEARCH THESE SPECIAL ITEMS ON EBAY, CRAIG'S LIST, REFERENCE BOOKS, OR APPRAISALS.								

← TOTAL FOR PAGE 79

YPG

CONTRIBUTION RECORD

For help with valuing your donations, see tips shown on page 78.	Gender	Qty	FMV better (high range)	Qty	FMV good (low range)	Your Total FMV	Estimate Original Purchase Price (Total)	Approx. Year Acquired
YOUR PAGE — TO DETERMINE FMV, RESEARCH THESE SPECIAL ITEMS ON EBAY, CRAIG'S LIST, REFERENCE BOOKS, OR APPRAISALS.									

← TOTAL FOR PAGE 80

CONTRIBUTION RECORD

For help with valuing your donations, see tips shown on page 78.	Gender	Qty	FMV better (high range)	Qty	FMV good (low range)	Your Total FMV	Estimate Original Purchase Price (Total)	Approx. Year Acquired
YOUR PAGE — TO DETERMINE FMV, RESEARCH THESE SPECIAL ITEMS ON EBAY, CRAIG'S LIST, REFERENCE BOOKS, OR APPRAISALS.									

← TOTAL FOR PAGE 81

YPG

CONTRIBUTION RECORD

For help with valuing your donations, see tips shown on page 78.	Gender	Qty	FMV better (high range)	Qty	FMV good (low range)	Your Total FMV	Estimate Original Purchase Price (Total)	Approx. Year Acquired
YOUR PAGE — TO DETERMINE FMV, RESEARCH THESE SPECIAL ITEMS ON EBAY, CRAIG'S LIST, REFERENCE BOOKS, OR APPRAISALS.								

← TOTAL FOR PAGE 82

CONTRIBUTION RECORD

For help with valuing your donations, see tips shown on page 78.	Gender	Qty	FMV better (high range)	Qty	FMV good (low range)	Your Total FMV	Estimate Original Purchase Price (Total)	Approx. Year Acquired
YOUR PAGE — TO DETERMINE FMV, RESEARCH THESE SPECIAL ITEMS ON EBAY, CRAIG'S LIST, REFERENCE BOOKS, OR APPRAISALS.								

← TOTAL FOR PAGE 83

YPG

CONTRIBUTION RECORD

For help with valuing your donations, see tips shown on page 78.	Gender	Qty	FMV better (high range)	Qty	FMV good (low range)	Your Total FMV	Estimate Original Purchase Price (Total)	Approx. Year Acquired
YOUR PAGE — TO DETERMINE FMV, RESEARCH THESE SPECIAL ITEMS ON EBAY, CRAIG'S LIST, REFERENCE BOOKS, OR APPRAISALS.									

← TOTAL FOR PAGE 84

CONTRIBUTION RECORD

For help with valuing your donations, see tips shown on page 78.	Gender	Qty	FMV better (high range)	Qty	FMV good (low range)	Your Total FMV	Estimate Original Purchase Price (Total)	Approx. Year Acquired
YOUR PAGE — TO DETERMINE FMV, RESEARCH THESE SPECIAL ITEMS ON EBAY, CRAIG'S LIST, REFERENCE BOOKS, OR APPRAISALS.								

← TOTAL FOR PAGE 85

YPG

DEDUCT IT! DEDUCT IT!
TOTALS PAGE 1 OF 4

Donation	A	B	C	D
Total From Page 19	$	$	$	$
Total From Page 20	$	$	$	$
Total From Page 21	$	$	$	$
Total From Page 22	$	$	$	$
Total From Page 23	$	$	$	$
Total From Page 24	$	$	$	$
Total From Page 25	$	$	$	$
Total From Page 26	$	$	$	$
Total From Page 27	$	$	$	$
Total From Page 28	$	$	$	$
Total From Page 29	$	$	$	$
Total From Page 30	$	$	$	$
Total From Page 31	$	$	$	$
Total From Page 32	$	$	$	$
Total From Page 33	$	$	$	$
Total From Page 34	$	$	$	$
Total From Page 35	$	$	$	$
Total From Page 36	$	$	$	$
Total From Page 37	$	$	$	$
Sub-Total	Donation A $	Donation B $	Donation C $	Donation D $

■ *DEDUCT IT! DEDUCT IT!*
TOTALS PAGE 2 OF 4

Donation	A	B	C	D
Total From Page 38	$	$	$	$
Total From Page 39	$	$	$	$
Total From Page 40	$	$	$	$
Total From Page 41	$	$	$	$
Total From Page 42	$	$	$	$
Total From Page 43	$	$	$	$
Total From Page 44	$	$	$	$
Total From Page 45	$	$	$	$
Total From Page 46	$	$	$	$
Total From Page 47	$	$	$	$
Total From Page 48	$	$	$	$
Total From Page 49	$	$	$	$
Total From Page 50	$	$	$	$
Total From Page 51	$	$	$	$
Total From Page 52	$	$	$	$
Total From Page 53	$	$	$	$
Total From Page 54	$	$	$	$
Total From Page 55	$	$	$	$
Total From Page 56	$	$	$	$
Sub-Total	Donation A $	Donation B $	Donation C $	Donation D $

■ *DEDUCT IT! DEDUCT IT!*
TOTALS PAGE 3 OF 4

Donation	A	B	C	D
Total From Page 57	$	$	$	$
Total From Page 58	$	$	$	$
Total From Page 59	$	$	$	$
Total From Page 60	$	$	$	$
Total From Page 61	$	$	$	$
Total From Page 62	$	$	$	$
Total From Page 63	$	$	$	$
Total From Page 64	$	$	$	$
Total From Page 65	$	$	$	$
Total From Page 66	$	$	$	$
Total From Page 67	$	$	$	$
Total From Page 68	$	$	$	$
Total From Page 69	$	$	$	$
Total From Page 70	$	$	$	$
Total From Page 71	$	$	$	$
Total From Page 72	$	$	$	$
Total From Page 73	$	$	$	$
Total From Page 74	$	$	$	$
Total From Page 75	$	$	$	$
Sub-Total	Donation A $	Donation B $	Donation C $	Donation D $

■ *DEDUCT IT! DEDUCT IT!*
TOTALS PAGE 4 OF 4

Donation	A	B	C	D
Total From Page 76	$	$	$	$
Total From Page 77	$	$	$	$
Total From Page 78	$	$	$	$
Total From Page 79	$	$	$	$
Total From Page 80	$	$	$	$
Total From Page 81	$	$	$	$
Total From Page 82	$	$	$	$
Total From Page 83	$	$	$	$
Total From Page 84	$	$	$	$
Total From Page 85	$	$	$	$
	Donation A	Donation B	Donation C	Donation D
Sub-Total	$	$	$	$

Total Amount Donated GRAND TOTAL A, B, C & D	$	$	$	$

CHARITY MILEAGE AND OUT-OF-POCKET EXPENSES

DATE	DESCRIPTION (attach receipts for costs)	Charitable MILEAGE	OUT-OF-POCKET EXPENSES for Charitable Service
			$
			$
			$
			$
			$
			$
			$
			$
			$
			$
			$
			$
			$
			$
			$
			$
			$
			$
			$
			$
			$
			$
			$
			$
			$
		Total Mileage/Costs	$

■ BEYOND THE CLOSET:
Other Types of Charitable Donations

If you itemize decuductions, a tax benefit equal to your marginal tax bracket is given to you for every dollar you contribute. Let's work the numbers backwards as an example:

Cash Contributions

Your Marginal Tax Bracket	Cash Contribution	Tax Savings	After-Tax Cost of Your Contribution
24%	$100	$24	$76
35%	$100	$35	$65
Charities accept credit cards — the donation is deductible in the year of the charge, even if you make the actual payment to the credit card company in the next year.			
Do you have a frequent flyer "miles" or other incentive program on your card? Get Miles *and* a Charitable Deduction at the same time.			

Appreciated Stock Contributions

An "appreciated stock or security" is a stock or bond that has grown in value since it was originally purchased. The Government has a program where you may be able to receive a greater tax advantage when you make gifts of appreciated stock — almost like saving taxes twice! Here's the explanation:

You may deduct the full market value of appreciated securities you've owned for over one year, and avoid any obligation to pay capital gains taxes. Here's an example to compare three ways to give - 1) if you wrote a check, 2) sold your stock and gave the proceeds to charity, or 3) "gifted" the appreciated stock:

In this situation, the person gifting is in a 35% (federal and state) tax bracket and 20% federal & state (if applicable) capital gains tax:

Gift Appreciated Stock

	Worse	Better	Best!
In this example, stock has a $500 cost basis*	Sell the Stock and Give the Cash	Write a check	Gift Appreciated Stock
Your Deduction	$3,000	$3,000	$3,000
Tax Savings @ 35%	$1,050	$1,050	$1,050
Capital Gains Tax	$500 <u>paid</u> by you	None	$500 <u>saved</u> by you
Bottomline your after-tax cost for a $3,000 gift	$2,450	$1,950	**$1,450**

*Basis = normally what you originally bought it for.
Based on 20% of $2,500 net capital gain

When you gift stock the charity can sell the shares and not pay taxes on the gain. Everybody wins!

Depreciated Stock Contributions

What if your stock depreciated? (When the price dropped below what you bought it for.) You should sell the stock yourself and donate the proceeds to charity. Then you can take a deduction for the capital loss as well as the charitable deduction.

Steps to Gifting Securities

Securities must be received by the charitable organization in the calendar year for which you intend to take the tax deduction (in other words, by December 31). It is best to allow six weeks for the transfer.

Suggested Process:

Consult with your tax and investment advisors about the amount and types of securities you wish to give.

Most charitable organizations have a special contact and phone number if you want to review the process or have any questions.

- If you are gifting mutual fund shares, the mutual fund will usually be happy to set up a courtesy account for the charity. Ask the mutual fund or your investment advisor to send the new account forms to the charitable fund. Then prepare a letter of instruction to the mutual fund, asking them to transfer the designated number of shares to the new charitable fund account, at no sales fee.

- If you hold your own stock certificates, you can safely transfer those certificates to the charities investment account. The charity will be happy to give you the name and the firm it is held under — examples include Charles Schwab and TD Ameritrade, etc.

- If you happen to have an investment account of your own at the same brokerage house, draft a letter of instruction to the firm, listing your account number, the number and type of securities you wish to transfer, and the instructions to transfer to the charities account.

- If you have an investment account at another brokerage, write a letter of instruction to your broker with your directions to transfer the securities to the charities account at their brokerage house.

Please consult your tax advisor regarding your specific legal and tax situation. Information herein is not legal or tax advice.

ATTACH/INSERT RECEIPTS/PHOTOS HERE

ATTACH/INSERT RECEIPTS/PHOTOS HERE

ATTACH/INSERT APPRAISALS HERE

NOTES

NOTES

ONLINE AND OTHER RESOURCES

IRS Publication 561, "Determining the Value of Donated Property" **irs.gov** *(Tax info for Contributors: irs.gov/charities)*	IRS Publication 526, "Charitable Organizations" In-depth explanation of how to claim your charitable contributions. **irs.gov**
Exempt Organizations Select Check With the online version, you can search for organizations by name to see if they qualify. **irs.gov/Charities-&-Non-Profits/Exempt-Organizations-Select-Check**	Goodwill Auctions The first Internet auction site created, owned and operated by a nonprofit organization **shopgoodwill.com**
American Society of Appraisers Find an appraiser with experience in IRS appraisals in your area. **appraisers.org**	Salvation Army® Valuation guide **salvationarmyusa.org**
Acceptable / Nonacceptable guidelines from various locations across the U.S. Not all charities have the same restrictions - please call ahead for large/bulky items! **donationtown.org**	Donating Computers **pickupplease.org** *(Electronics and other donations accepted)* **computerswithcauses.org** **crc.org** **dellreconnect.com** *(Any brand computer accepted, drop-off locations listed by Zip Code)*
DeductItTracker.com	

CHARITY VERIFICATION TRACKER

Charity Name		☐ Receipt	Donation
Address		☐ Photograph(s) Mark B	**A**
Donation Date:	Amount:	☐ Charity Donation Attendant Initial to verify donation:	

Charity Name		☐ Receipt	Donation
Address		☐ Photograph(s) Mark B	**B**
Donation Date:	Amount:	☐ Charity Donation Attendant Initial to verify donation:	

Charity Name		☐ Receipt	Donation
Address		☐ Photograph(s) Mark B	**C**
Donation Date:	Amount:	☐ Charity Donation Attendant Initial to verify donation:	

Charity Name		☐ Receipt	Donation
Address		☐ Photograph(s) Mark B	**D**
Donation Date:	Amount:	☐ Charity Donation Attendant Initial to verify donation: